Who Comes?

Who Comes?

by Deborah Chandra ■ Illustrations by Katie Lee

SIERRA CLUB BOOKS FOR CHILDREN

SAN FRANCISCO

The Sierra Club, founded in 1892 by John Muir, has devoted itself to the study and
protection of the earth's scenic and ecological resources — mountains, wetlands, woodlands,
wild shores and rivers, deserts and plains. The publishing program of the Sierra Club offers
books to the public as a nonprofit educational service in the hope that they may enlarge the
public's understanding of the Club's basic concerns. The point of view expressed in each
book, however, does not necessarily represent that of the Club. The Sierra Club has some
sixty chapters in the United States and in Canada. For information about how you may
participate in its programs to preserve wilderness and the quality of life, please address
inquiries to Sierra Club, 730 Polk Street, San Francisco, CA 94109.

First Edition

Library of Congress Cataloging-in-Publication Data

Chandra, Deborah.
     Who comes? / Deborah Chandra ; illustrations by Katie Lee. — 1st ed.
        p. cm.
     Summary: An illustrated poem tells how various animals come to a
watering hole on the African plains, unaware that a lion is on the prowl.
     ISBN 0-87156-407-6 (hardcover)
      1. Children's poetry, American. 2. Animals — Juvenile poetry.
3. Africa — Juvenile poetry. [1. Animals — Poetry. 2. Africa — Poetry
3. American poetry.] I. Lee, Katie, 1942- ill. II. Title.
PS3553.H2716W46 1995
811'.54 — dc20   94-47193

Art direction by Susan Lu Bussard
Book and jacket design by Big Fish Books

Printed in Hong Kong on acid-free paper made entirely from tree-farm wood.
No chlorine was used in the making of this paper.

10 9 8 7 6 5 4 3 2 1

To my sister, Rachel
— DC

To Morgan
— KL

Someone comes to the waterhole,
glistening in the evening sun,
to cool his paws and wet his tongue.
Who comes? Who?

The lion comes.

Soft haunting songs of cuckoos rise.
The lion sees with golden eyes
someone move among the reeds.
Who moves? Who?

A wildebeest.

The sun goes down. Shadows grow.

The wildebeest thinks he's alone.

He slowly wades and stoops to drink.

He does not see the lion creep.

Beneath a thorn tree's tangled bough,
someone hears the cuckoos sing
an ancient chant of chase and hunt.
Who hears? Who?

A waterbuck.
He rubs his horns, then lifts his lips
to nibble at the green reed tips.
He shakes his head, stamps his feet.
He does not see the lion creep.

A shadow slides between the trees.
Someone softly stirs the leaves.
Twilight rides upon his back.
Who comes? Who?

A lone giraffe.
The water laps his legs. He sees
his shadow caught in waterweeds
while leaning his long neck to drink.
He does not see the lion creep.

Hidden by the warm black night,
someone steps along the mud,
leaving hoofprints one by one.
Who comes? Who?

A zebra comes.
He sniffs the air. A shivering flow
of stars floats on the waterhole.
The zebra dips his mouth to drink.
He does not see the lion creep.

The rising moon shines broad and bright,
casting down a flood of light.
From the plains jackals call.
The lion creeps on silent paws.

Closer . . . closer, crouching low,
with heavy breath. His gold eyes glow.
Beneath the wild and silent sky,
the lion leaps. The zebra dies.

Hoofbeats drum upon the ground,
then stillness. Soon, with rustling sounds,
like ghosts in moonlight through the reeds,
animals return to drink.

Someone comes to the waterhole
to cool his paws and wet his tongue.
Along the muddy edge he moves.
The cuckoos cry. Who comes? Who?